L
3398

Lynx

Lynx

by Jost Schneider
edited by Sylvia A. Johnson

A Carolrhoda Nature Watch Book

 Carolrhoda Books, Inc./Minneapolis

Thanks to Michael DonCarlos, Fur-Bearer Specialist, Minnesota Department of Natural Resources, for his assistance with this book

Additional photographs courtesy of: © Kent and Donna Dannen, pp. 40, 43; © Michael H. Francis, pp. 4, 9, 38, 41 (both), 42, 44. Illustration p. 8 by Laura Westlund, © Carolrhoda Books, Inc.

This edition first published 1995 by Carolrhoda Books, Inc. Original edition copyright © 1991 by Kinderbuchverlag Reich Luzern AG, Lucerne, Switzerland, under the title LUCHSE: DIE HEIMLICHEN WALDBEWOHNER. Translated from the German by Amy Gelman. Adapted by Carolrhoda Books, Inc. All additional material supplied for this edition copyright © 1995 by Carolrhoda Books, Inc.

This book is available in two editions:
Library binding by Carolrhoda Books, Inc.
Soft cover by First Avenue Editions, 1997
c/o The Lerner Group
241 First Avenue North
Minneapolis, Minnesota 55401

LIBRARY OF CONGRESS CATALOGING-IN-PUBLICATION DATA

Schneider, Jost, 1950–
  [Luchse. English]
  Lynx / by Jost Schneider ; edited by Sylvia A. Johnson.
    p. cm.
  "A Carolrhoda nature watch book."
  Includes index.
  ISBN 0-87614-844-5 (lib. bdg.)
  ISBN 1-57505-063-3 (pbk.)
  1. Lynx — Juvenile literature. [1. Lynx.] I. Johnson, Sylvia A. II. Title.
QL737.C23S34513 1995
599.74'428 — dc20   94-2119

Manufactured in the United States of America
2 3 4 5 6 7 – JR – 02 01 00 99 98 97

CONTENTS

On a cold winter morning, the dense forest is silent. Snow covers the ground, and the only sound that can be heard is the sighing of wind in the trees.

The forest seems empty, for most of its inhabitants have taken shelter from the severe cold. But one animal still prowls the trails, alert to the snap of a twig or the crunch of a hoof in the snow.

If you are lucky, you might get a glimpse of this furry, long-legged animal through the trees. Standing perfectly still, it seems to be looking back at you. Then, with a sudden movement, it bounds away and disappears into the depths of the forest.

All lynxes have tufts of long black hair on the tips of their ears.

MEET THE LYNX

You have just spotted a lynx, one of the most mysterious members of the cat family. Compared to many of its relatives, the lynx is not very well known. Everyone has seen movies and television programs about lions, leopards, and tigers. But the shy and secretive lynx is not often captured on film.

Lynxes are medium-sized cats, quite a bit smaller than the so-called big cats (lions, tigers, leopards, and cheetahs) but larger than little wild cats like the caracal or margay. They have soft, thick fur that is usually some shade of yellow-ish or grayish brown. Lynx fur is often marked with darker spots or lines. But the cats do not have distinctive markings like leopards, cheetahs, and tigers.

One way to recognize a lynx is by looking at its ears. All **species**, or kinds, have tufts of long black hairs on the tips of their large ears. Most lynxes also have a kind of ruff or collar of long hair around their necks and under their chins. Long legs, big feet, and short tails are some of the other physical features shared by the different species of lynxes.

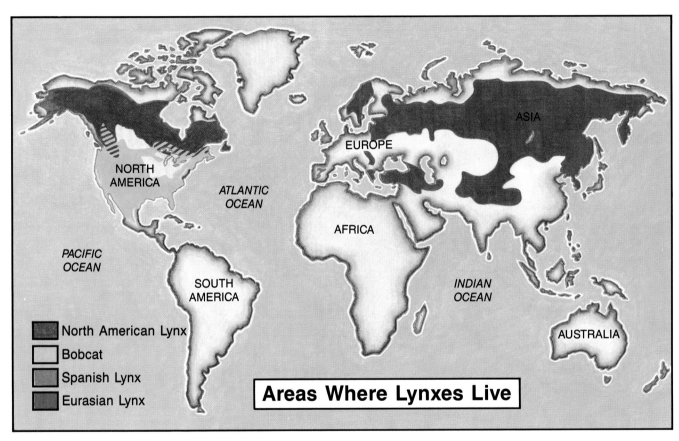

This maps shows where the different species of lynxes live.

One important thing sets the lynx apart from other members of the cat family. Lynxes make their homes in several different parts of the world.

Today most kinds of wild cats are found in only one region. The lion lives in Africa, while the jaguar prowls the forests of Central and South America. You will find tigers and snow leopards only in Asia. But the lynx is at home on three different continents.

One species of lynx lives in large areas of Asia and in some parts of Europe. This cat is usually called the Eurasian lynx; its scientific name is *Lynx lynx*. The Spanish lynx, *Lynx pardinus*, is found

The Eurasian lynx (left) *and the Canada lynx* (below) *live in different parts of the world, but the two cats have a lot in common.*

only in southwestern Spain. Another lynx species is a native of North America. Its scientific name is *Lynx canadensis,* and Canada is its home. A closely related animal, the bobcat (*Lynx rufus*), is found throughout the United States and in northern Mexico.

Because lynxes live in such different parts of the world, their habits are not exactly the same. The cats may hunt different animals for food or have their young at different times of year. But most lynxes share a basic way of living. In this book, we will follow the trail of the lynx and discover how the cat makes its way in the world.

TRACKING THE EURASIAN LYNX

The first place we will look for a lynx is in the country of Switzerland. Eurasian lynxes live here, in forested, mountainous regions far from the crowded cities.

As it roams through the forest, the lynx follows trails made by deer or even those used by skiers. If you walk along one of these trails, you might see signs that a lynx has been there before you.

Here is one sign—a tuft of soft fur caught on a blackberry bush. Farther along is a footprint about the size of a human fist. There are no claw marks because the lynx, like almost all cats, pulls its claws in when it walks.

A footprint and a tuft of fur on a bush are signs that a lynx is in the area.

Just like a domestic cat, the lynx works hard at keeping itself clean.

If you follow the tracks of the lynx, you might be lucky enough to spot the cat and observe it in its natural surroundings. How does a lynx spend its day? It does many of the same things that all cats do.

One important activity is keeping clean. Just like a pet cat, the lynx spends a lot of time licking its coat with its rough tongue. It has a very flexible spine and can reach almost all parts of its body. The lynx washes its face by scrubbing it with a wet paw.

Above: *Stretching and yawning after a nap, a lynx displays its impressive canine teeth.* **Left:** *Like a house cat using a litter box, a lynx covers its feces with snow.*

Another important daily task for the lynx is making sure that its claws are sharp. Just as a pet cat scrapes its claws on a scratching post (or the living room sofa), the lynx scratches on trees or pieces of wood. This action pulls off the worn outer layer of the claw and exposes the sharp new layer underneath.

Scratching also serves another purpose. By making marks on trees or logs, a lynx leaves a message that lets other lynxes know of its presence. This is one of the many ways that the cats keep in touch with each other.

ON THE TRAIL OF THE HUNTER

Of all the lynx's daily activities, the most important is hunting. Like all cats, lynxes are **predators** that kill other animals for food. They are expert hunters whose lives depend on finding **prey.**

Like most cats, the lynx hunts by sneaking up quietly on prey animals and then attacking. As the Eurasian lynx prowls through the forest of Switzerland, it listens for the sounds other

Lynxes use their acute sense of hearing to locate prey.

animals make. The cat's hearing is very sharp, and it depends on this sense and sight, rather than smell, to find prey.

When the lynx hears a suspicious sound, it begins to move toward it, keeping low to the ground. Stopping to listen, hiding behind trees and clumps of grass, and then moving forward again, it tracks the animal. When it is close enough, it leaps on the prey.

Moving silently through the forest, a lynx tracks its prey.

In Switzerland, the Eurasian lynx hunts several different kinds of prey. One of the most common is the roe deer (below), which is similar to the white-tailed deer of North America. The lynx also kills chamoix (opposite), antelope-like animals that are native to the Swiss Alps. Sometimes the cat's diet includes smaller animals like hares (right), woodchucks, foxes, and squirrels.

Broad, furry feet help the lynx to run over snow.

Winter hunting brings some special problems for the lynx, and also some advantages. The cat can easily be seen against the white snow, and there is no grass or other vegetation to hide in.

18

If chamoix get a headstart, they can easily outrun a lynx. The cat catches its prey only one out of six times.

While stalking, it has to conceal itself behind rocks or in depressions in the ground.

But the lynx has no problem moving over the snow. Its feet are large—about four inches (10 centimeters) wide—and covered with fur. Like snowshoes, they keep the cat from sinking into the snow.

Despite the advantage of its snowshoe feet, the lynx cannot chase its prey for very long. Like most cats, it does not have the endurance for long-distance running. If a deer or a chamois hears the lynx before it gets close enough to pounce, the animal runs away. The cat quickly gives up the chase. Only about one hunt out of six ends up with the lynx catching its prey.

To use its sharp back teeth, a lynx has to turn its head to one side.

A lynx usually kills a small animal by biting the neck with its sharp canine teeth and cutting the spinal cord. When the prey is larger, the cat holds the animal's throat until it suffocates.

After killing an animal, the lynx begins to eat it on the spot. The cat uses its razor-sharp back teeth, called **carnassials,** to cut into the prey's flesh. Turning its head sideways, it brings these teeth together like the blades of scissors.

20

After the lynx has eaten its fill, it carefully covers up the rest of the prey with grass, leaves, dirt, or snow. It does this to hide its food from other predators like foxes, eagles, or bears.

The lynx stays hidden near its food supply, resting during the day and feeding in the evening. Eventually almost all of the prey is eaten. All that is left is the animal's head, feet, hide, and large bones. The lynx doesn't let anything edible go to waste.

One deer or chamois will feed a lynx for about five to seven days. Then the predator has to hunt again.

After feeding, the lynx covers up the rest of its prey. The cat stays hidden nearby, resting and eating until almost everything is gone.

FAMILY LIFE

The Eurasian lynx, like most cats, is a solitary animal. Each adult lynx has its own **home range**, where it hunts and lives alone. These ranges vary in size, depending on how many prey animals there are in the area. In Switzerland, they can be as small as 20 square miles (about 50 square kilometers) or as large as 200 square miles (about 500 square kilometers).

Generally, male lynxes have larger ranges than female lynxes. And a single male's home range often overlaps the ranges of several different females.

Lynxes mark the boundaries of their home ranges with signposts. They spray strong-smelling urine on rocks, trees, or stumps. These scent messages usually tell other lynxes to keep out. But when the time for mating comes, the odors help male and female lynxes to find each other.

For most Eurasian lynxes, mating season comes in early spring. It is only at this time of year that female lynxes are able to mate and have young. The scent

Male and female lynxes are fairly similar in appearance. The male (left) *is usually a little larger and more powerful than the female* (right).

marks that the females leave contain special "messages" that let males know about their condition. When a male lynx picks up these signals, he starts roaming around his home range, looking for possible partners.

A male lynx sits on a branch watching a female hidden under the roots of a tree.

Left: *Two courting lynxes enjoy each other's company.* Below: *The female lynx crouches down and raises her tail to let the male know she is ready to mate.*

Before they can mate, a male and female lynx need to get acquainted. Each has to make sure that its partner has friendly intentions and is not going to attack. To get to know each other, the cats go through a period of **courtship**.

During their courtship, the two lynxes may chase each other or even go hunting together. They spend a lot of time sniffing and licking each other's bodies or gently butting heads together. Sometimes they just lie side by side and survey their surroundings.

After several days of courtship, the two lynxes finally mate. During the act

During mating, the male holds the female by the back of her neck. After mating is completed, the two cats separate quickly, hissing and snarling at each other.

of mating, the male grips the female by the skin on the back of her neck. (Most male cats do this, perhaps to prevent the females from attacking them.)

The lynxes may mate several times before the male finally leaves to look for other partners. A female lynx usually mates with only one male.

YOUNG LYNXES

About 10 weeks after mating, the female lynx will give birth to her young. She will raise them alone, without the help of the father. Male lynxes play no role in family life.

During her pregnancy, the female looks for a good place to shelter her young. A cave, a hollow log, or a space under an uprooted tree makes a safe den for the mother and the young lynxes.

A female Eurasian lynx usually has from one to five **kittens**. Like most cats,

This female lynx has made a den under the roots of an old tree.

the little lynxes are born with their eyes closed. They are tiny creatures and depend completely on their mother for warmth, food, and protection.

26

For the first few days of their lives, the female lynx stays with her young constantly. Finally, hunger forces her to leave them for short periods while she hunts. This is a dangerous time because the helpless kittens could be discovered by foxes or other predators.

To keep her young safe, the female lynx sometimes moves them to another spot. She gently picks each kitten up by the loose skin on the back of its neck. Then she carries it to the new hiding place. When they are being carried in this way, the kittens stay very quiet and do not wiggle or try to get away.

Above: *Hidden among the leaves, a female nurses her young.* Below: *A lynx mother carries a kitten by the loose skin on the back of its neck.*

Lynx kittens grow up quickly. When they are two weeks old, their eyes open. At this age, they can keep themselves warm, so they don't have to stay huddled close to their mother.

But the female will remain their main source of food for the first three or four months of their lives. Her milk makes a nourishing diet that gets the young lynxes off to a good start.

By the time the kittens are six weeks old, they are following their mother on short trips away from the den. When she hunts, they stay at home. The kittens are able to eat some meat now, and the female brings them pieces of animals that she has killed. When they are a little older, she will take them with her to feed on prey.

Young lynxes are good at climbing trees.

A female lynx takes good care of her kittens, keeping them safe and well groomed.

As the young lynxes continue to grow, they become more active and curious. They explore the area around their den, learning about their surroundings. Of course, they always come back to their mother for food and comfort.

With their sharp claws, the kittens are good tree climbers. They scamper up trunks and over fallen logs. When they grow up, they will not spend much time in trees. Adult lynxes usually climb trees only to escape danger. They don't leap on prey animals from trees, as people used to think.

31

Like most young cats, lynx kittens spend some of their time playing games. One kitten will sneak up quietly on another and pounce. The young animals chase each other and play at fighting.

All these games allow the kittens to practice the skills they will need as adult predators. The young lynxes have the in- stinct to kill animals for food, but they don't know exactly how to do the job. They have to learn hunting methods by practice and observation.

Like most female cats, a lynx mother helps her young to become good hunters. She sometimes brings small half-dead animals like hares or squirrels back to

When this lynx kitten grows up, it will have long legs and big feet, just like its mother.

the den so that the kittens can practice stalking and killing. This kind of "play" might seem cruel to us, but it is an important part of learning to be a predator.

When the young lynxes are about six to eight months old, they will go with their mother when she hunts. Sometimes the whole family tracks an animal together. If the prey escapes one lynx, another one may catch it. Through this kind of cooperative hunting, a young lynx gets food that it might not be able to catch by itself.

Above: *During the time that they are learning to hunt, lynx kittens still depend on their mother for food.* Right: *When a kitten gets unruly, its mother hisses and gives it a swat with her paw.*

When the young lynxes are about one year old, the time comes for them to leave home. Their mother is ready to mate again and produce another family. She doesn't want her almost-grown young hanging around anymore.

Each of the young lynxes has to find its own home range. A female lynx usually doesn't go far away. She often establishes her range near that of her mother. A young male, on the other hand, travels a long distance from his birth family to

These young lynxes are almost grown and will soon go off to start their own lives.

find a range of his own.

Going off on their own is dangerous for the young lynxes. Some of them may wander across roads and be killed by cars. Others may have trouble finding a place to live and enough food to eat.

If they survive, the lynxes will soon start families of their own. The females are able to have young when they are 1 year old. Males have to be at least 2 years old before they can reproduce. If they're lucky, lynxes may live for 10 to 12 years.

THE RETURN OF THE EURASIAN LYNX

The Eurasian lynx used to live in many countries of Europe. By the mid-1900s, however, it had almost become extinct in this part of the world. Hunting and trapping had seriously reduced the lynx population. Only in Norway and Sweden and in the European part of the Soviet Union were lynxes found in any numbers.

Then in the 1970s, some people decided to try and bring the lynx back to parts of Switzerland, Austria, Germany, and a few other countries of western Europe. Eurasian lynxes were brought from areas where they were abundant and released in the forested mountains of these countries.

The transplanted lynxes adjusted well to their new surroundings. But there were problems. In their search for prey, lynxes sometimes killed sheep and goats. This caused hardship for the owners of these domestic animals.

Hunters were also disturbed by the activities of the lynxes. They complained that the cats killed too many deer and chamoix for food, and there weren't enough animals left for them to hunt.

In the 1970s, the Eurasian lynx was reintroduced in Switzerland and a few other countries of western Europe.

Despite these problems, the lynxes seem to have become established in Switzerland and in a few other areas. Whether they can survive there depends mainly on the actions of people.

THE LYNX IN NORTH AMERICA

Lynxes are fairly abundant in North America. The Canada lynx lives in almost all the provinces of Canada and in the state of Alaska. There are also some lynxes in the U. S. states along the Canadian border. In North America, lynxes are not in danger of extinction, but they have some problems of their own.

The North American lynx has a lot in common with the Eurasian lynx. In fact, many scientists believe that this species of cat originally migrated from Asia to North America thousands of years ago. It probably crossed the land bridge that linked the two continents in ancient times.

A Eurasian lynx female may have one to five kittens. A Canada lynx usually has no more than four young at one time.

Like its close cousin, the Canada lynx has a home range where it hunts and lives alone. It moves easily over the snow on the same enormous, furry feet. Female Canada lynxes usually bear two to four kittens and teach them to be good hunters before sending them off on their own.

The Canada lynx is only half the size of its Eurasian cousin.

There are two important differences between the Canada lynx and the Eurasian lynx. One is size. Most Canada lynxes are only half as large as their Eurasian relatives. An average adult male weighs around 22 pounds (about 10 kilograms) rather than 44 pounds (about 20 kilograms).

The other difference between the two cats is the prey they catch. Because Canada lynxes are fairly small, they are not usually able to kill animals as large as deer. Instead, their main prey is a member of the rabbit family, the snowshoe hare. To keep well fed, a Canada lynx has to catch one hare almost every day.

Scientists have discovered that there is a very close relationship between the lynx and the snowshoe hare. Lynxes depend on hares for food, and they don't easily switch to other prey. This means that when snowshoe hares are scarce, lynxes get hungry.

Studies have shown that the population of snowshoe hares in an area usually goes through a kind of cycle. About every 10 years or so, disease or lack of food causes many adult hares to die before reproducing. When this happens, the hare population begins to drop.

The snowshoe hare wears different coats in summer and in winter. Its white winter coat helps it to blend in with its surroundings.

When snowshoe hares are scarce, lynx kittens may not get enough to eat.

When the number of snowshoe hares decreases in an area, the lynx population soon falls too. Female lynxes do not have enough food to feed their kittens. If food is really scarce, females may not reproduce at all. Without enough food, many adult lynxes die of starvation.

During a time of food shortage, some lynxes move away from their home ranges. The cats have been known to travel for long distances in search of prey. Hunger can even drive them into cities. Lynxes have been seen in the outskirts of large Canadian cities like Edmonton and Winnipeg and even as far south as Minneapolis, Minnesota.

Far away from their home ranges, wandering lynxes are in dangerous territory. Many of them are hit by cars or shot by people.

Back home, in the area affected by the hare shortage, many lynxes also die, but some usually survive. The hare population gradually recovers, and as it does, so do the predators. When enough food is available, the young lynxes that are born have a good chance of living to be adults. During years when there are a lot of hares, a female lynx may produce three to six kittens instead of two to four.

In these good times, the number of lynxes rises. But eventually, the hare population begins to drop again, and the whole cycle starts over.

Some lynxes travel great distances to find food.

THE LYNX'S FUR COAT

Like many cats, the lynx is hunted and trapped for its soft, thick fur.

Like many members of the cat family, the lynx is hunted and trapped for its fur. Soft, warm lynx fur is used to make coats and jackets. As many as 40 lynxes may have to be killed to produce one coat.

Today, international laws control the trade in the fur of most cats, including the lynx. In the 1970s, the Convention of International Trade in Endangered Species established lists of cats that were endangered by the fur trade. The most threatened were some of the striped and spotted cats, for example, the tiger, the cheetah, and the ocelot. International agreements outlawed the legal trade in the fur of these cats.

The lynx was not considered to be threatened. It was placed on a list of cats that could be trapped if the trade in their fur was closely monitored.

After the trade in striped and spotted cat fur was made illegal, however, some fur traders decided that lynx fur would make a good substitute. They particularly wanted the soft, spotted fur on the cat's belly. As a result, the number of lynxes killed for their fur increased dramatically during the 1980s.

Despite this increase, the lynx seems to be hanging on. So far, the lynx populations in North America, in the Scandinavian countries, and in the former Soviet Union have not been seriously affected by trapping.

But scientists are concerned about long-range effects on the Canada lynx. If too many lynxes are trapped during a low point in the population cycle, the lynx could be wiped out in certain areas. As is true with so many other animals, the future of the lynx may depend on the actions and decisions of people.

GLOSSARY

carnassials: sharp teeth in the back of a cat's jaws used to cut up prey. The carnassials on one side of the mouth work together like blades of a scissors to slice flesh.

courtship: a series of actions or behaviors that prepare animals for mating. When lynxes court, they hunt together and lick and sniff each other's bodies.

home range: an area in which one animal lives and hunts. Most animals mark the boundaries of their ranges with urine and other strong-smelling substances. Among lynxes, the home range of a female often overlaps that of a male.

kittens: the name used for baby lynxes and the young of other small and medium-sized cats. The young of large cats like lions are called cubs.

predator: an animal that kills other animals for food

prey: an animal that is killed and eaten by a predator

species: a group of animals that have many characteristics in common. Eurasian lynxes belong to a species called *Lynx lynx*. The North American lynx is in a different but closely related species, *Lynx canadensis*.

INDEX

ABOUT THE AUTHOR/PHOTOGRAPHER

Jost Schneider has been fascinated by nature since he was a child. His career as a photographer and filmmaker began when he did a study of roe deer that was awarded first prize by a youth organization in his native Switzerland. After becoming a professional photographer, Jost produced documentary films on subjects such as national parks and the life of the red fox. His nature photographs have been featured in many books and magazines, and he has written several books for young people. Jost says that taking pictures of the lynx for this book required a lot of luck, time, and patience. Thanks to his hard work, readers can get a rare look at the secretive cat in its natural habitat.